ISBN: 978-0-9952573-2-0
Cover design and layout: Abria Mattina.

Introduction

While reading Life Reboot, you will have a chance to go on your own inner journey. When moving through the chapters, go at a pace that feels right for you. Some chapters may cause you to reflect for longer periods of time than others.

This workbook is your companion to the Life Reboot book. The exercises are designed to help you reflect and to tune into your own inner wisdom for guidance along the way. Some exercises may take a few minutes and others could take longer, requiring deeper introspection. Allow yourself to be curious and to ask questions.

For many of the exercises, we will be using the techniques of brainstorming and freewriting. Brainstorming is a popular technique used in groups to spark creativity by writing out ideas in the form of spontaneous lists – you can brainstorm by yourself as well. Writers and others, commonly use freewriting - where you write for a continuous amount of time (anywhere from 2-10 minutes) without any regard for spelling and grammar - to help overcome blocks of self-criticism or perfection. Your journal entries don't have to be perfect. Don't worry about censoring your answers out of fear of somebody reading them.

If you get to a point where you feel you have nothing to write, then write about the fact you have nothing to write – just keep the pen moving. I've solved many problems this way by writing a question in my journal, then free writing. When I'm not looking for a solution, it often comes out in my writing.

By completing the exercises, you will connect to your soul and gain more clarity on your dreams and desires. You will learn about common roadblocks that are holding you back from moving forward in your life. Finally you will be guided towards taking action so that your dreams are no longer fantasies in your head, but will become your reality.

Happy writing!

Sarah Wall

Exercise One

On the following page, you will write a letter to your younger self. You may write whatever you wish and the letter can be as long as you choose. Use the following as a guideline and feel free to elaborate.

1. Write down today's date and your current age.

2. Dear (insert your name),

3. Note the age of your younger self or a period in your life that you are addressing.

4. What do you want to say to your younger self? Write down the first thing that comes to mind.

5. What wisdom would you like to share with your younger self? Perhaps choose one or two topics, rather than writing about everything you have learned since then.

6. Sign it with love. Keep the letter in a safe place. You may wish to read your letter again when you have finished this book, or at some point in the future when you are feeling reflective. Notice how you feel when you are reading the wisdom you have shared with your younger self.

Congratulations! You've completed your first journaling exercise.

Dear _____ Date: _____ Age: _____

_____

_____

_____

_____

_____

_____

_____

_____

_____

_____

_____

_____

_____

_____

_____

_____

_____

_____

Exercise Two

For a minimum of one week, spend time getting to know your inner world through freewriting for five to ten minutes a day. I encourage you to try this for at least one week in order to get into the habit of daily writing. If you are able to continue journaling for the time that you are reading this book, it will be helpful for you to go back and reflect upon your state at different stages of your journey. The frustrations that you are experiencing today might be quite different than the ones you are facing by the time you are finished the book.

1. **Make a commitment to yourself**

   Today is the perfect day to start. It's the first step on your journey. You can't get this wrong and you can always go back to revisit and elaborate on your writing at the end of the week. Say it out loud: "I _____, commit to spending _____ minutes each day to freewriting, for seven days." Write this down, sign it and date it.

2. **Find a consistent time each day and a place where it will be quiet so you can focus**

   This could be first thing in the morning before everyone else wakes up and before you start going about your day. If you're a night owl then set aside time in the evening. Consistency is key.

3. **Don't allow yourself to get distracted**

   Your household chores, phone and cat can wait. We're very good at creating distractions when we don't want to do something, even if it's for our greater good. For example, my apartment was always spotless right before exam time in school! If you really can't help yourself, then get all of those distractions out of the way today: clean your house, run your errands and then start writing.

4. **Take a few moments to relax yourself before you begin.**

   Whether that's sitting quietly, taking a few deep breaths, or making a cup of tea to accompany you while you write, make this part of your daily ritual.

5. **Forget about the outcome**

   Don't worry about your writing style or spelling, as you won't be sharing this with anyone. Don't be afraid of what might be revealed for fear of uncovering your deepest, darkest secrets, or fear of offending someone. This is a process of self discovery and the point of this exercise is get you in the habit of taking action and to begin to release your inner thoughts onto paper, to see what lies underneath and for reflection later on.

If you're stuck for inspiration, start by writing out a question or a statement you've been pondering, or think about how any of the signs of discord show up in your life, and then allow your pen to reveal the answers through your writing.

Sometimes it's enough to get the creative juices flowing to describe what you did the prior day or to write out what you are looking forward to today. I encourage you to come up with your own questions or statements. If you're feeling stuck, here are some examples of statements to help you get started:

1. The one thing that makes me feel sad is _____

2. I would describe my perfect day as _____

3. I feel most angry when _____

4. Today I am most looking forward to _____

5. I feel most happy when I am _____

Day One

Day Two

_____

_____

_____

_____

_____

_____

_____

_____

_____

_____

_____

_____

_____

_____

_____

_____

_____

Day Three

Day Four

Day Five

Day Six

Day Seven

Go back and read what you have written and notice if you spot any patterns in your writing. Silence the inner critic and do not be concerned about spelling or grammar or if the words even make sense. Imagine looking at the content objectively as if you are reading someone else's words.

1. Is there something there that you have written about more than once that may be trying to get your attention?
2. Are there any particular words that jump out at you?
3. Write down what you notice on the following page.

If you really enjoyed this exercise, I recommend you continue freewriting daily for the entire time you are reading this book or even longer, as it helps to unload the mind first thing in the morning or at the end of the day. If you didn't enjoy this exercise, I also recommend that you continue freewriting daily for the entire time you are reading this book. We often resist the things we most need to learn or change about ourselves. Maybe you can write about why you don't like freewriting.

Reflections

Exercise Three

Before you go down the path of reaching out to your find your tribe, let's take some time to visualize the type of people you imagine surrounding yourself with. Whether you wish to brainstorm by writing a list, or continue with freewriting, is up to you.

1. With a gentle smile on your face, close your eyes and take a few deep breaths. Think of a time when you felt on top of the world, when you felt fully supported and free to express the real you, without any judgment. As you breathe in, allow that feeling to expand throughout your body and enjoy the expansion it brings. As you breathe out, allow your body to become more relaxed.

2. If nothing comes to mind, use your imagination to feel what it would be like to be totally free and happy and surrounded by people who support you in your growth.

3. After a few minutes, or when it feels right, open your eyes and write down some of the sensations you felt in your body, what images or words came to mind during that exercise.

4. Go a little deeper and describe the qualities of the person, or people, who were there with you during the visualization. By performing this visualization you are calling into existence your future tribe.

Now it's time to take action. What's the first smallest step you can take to seek out and connect with your tribe? I challenge you take this first step within one week from today.

Reflections

Reflections

Exercise Four

In the space below, revisit and write responses to similar questions that you were reflecting upon earlier. Notice if anything is getting in the way of your writing, such as a tiny voice that's telling you it's not possible, or that your dreams are crazy. The more you pay attention to the voices in your head, the more you will begin to decipher between those voices that are there to encourage you and those that are peppered with doubt. Try to ignore the negative, doubtful voices and keep writing.

1. What are your dreams?
2. Imagine there are no limits and you can pursue anything, what would it be?
3. What legacy do you wish to leave behind?
4. What is preventing you from taking the first step?

Reflections

Reflections

Reflections

Reflections

Exercise Five

In *Life Reboot* I described how I had created a vision board that was filled with images of beautiful destinations and had a strong theme of travel. I have created a few different vision boards since then. Now is the time for you to take action by creating your vision board. Creating a vision board is a way to put your intentions onto paper and it's an activity you can do alone or with a group of friends.

I gathered a small group of women together at my home for a potluck dinner, for the purpose of creating our vision boards together. We met a few times for more potlucks throughout the year to check in on our progress. It was really interesting to share our successes and funny stories and also to see what had changed since our last meeting. The vision board is meant to serve as an inspiration, to guide you towards what your heart deeply desires.

Whether you are doing this activity solo, or with friends, you will need to gather some supplies such as; old magazines or newspapers, scissors, glue, tape, cardboard or bristol board, markers, stickers and possibly string or glitter – whatever crafts you have on hand.

1. Begin to leaf through the magazines and cut out images and words that resonate with you, things that make you feel happy. Don't worry about what the final vision board will look like at this time – it's a creative process.

2. Once you feel you have enough content, you then begin to layout the images and words on your board. Maybe you want to write a key statement or message in the centre – something that you want to bring into your life? Write this message as if it's already here, not in the future tense.

3. Continue to organize and create your board by gluing or taping the magazine cuttings and

adding whatever creative flair you like – there is no wrong way to do this. Take as long as you need until you feel your board is complete.

4. If you're in a group, it's nice to share your board once everyone has finished (if you feel comfortable), maybe talking about the primary theme or why you chose certain images.

5. Place your vision board somewhere prominent, where you will see it every day. Spend a few moments with it each day taking in in visually and observing the feelings that arise.

When you view your vision board, imagine that everything on there is already here and now. Notice if feelings of lack come up when you are looking at your board. For example, my vision board that was filled with images of beautiful beaches and lush jungles, if I was looking at it and feeling that I would never get to visit those places and it was all just a pipe dream, then chances are I would never have gone to places like Fiji and Malaysia and Indonesia, because of my limiting beliefs. However, when I was viewing my board, it was always with feelings of happiness and excitement and an eagerness that visiting these places was just around the corner, even if I had no idea how I would get there or when it would happen. I could imagine myself on the beach, I could smell the salty sea air, and I could feel the humidity of the lush rainforest.

By going through this feeling and vision process daily, you might be surprised at what starts showing up in your life. The items on your board may not manifest exactly the way you have anticipated, nor is the timing fixed. Be open to possibility and trust in the power of your intention.

Exercise Six

You can practice tuning into your gut instinct right now, wherever you are, as you are reading this book. Once you learn your signals, you will be better able to understand yourself and read your reactions to other people in various situations.

1. If you're not already sitting down, take a moment to make yourself comfortable, sitting up nice and tall with your shoulders slightly drawn back opening your chest. Ensure your feet are firmly planted on the floor if you are sitting in a chair.

2. Take a few slow, deep breaths in and out, to help relax yourself and allow your belly to feel soft.

3. Notice if you feel tension in your body. If you're feeling tightness, take a few more deep breaths, setting the intention that you will become more relaxed with each exhale.

4. Now, out loud, verbally make a *false* statement about yourself that is not emotionally charged. For example, since I'm a woman living in Canada, I would say "I am a man," or "I live in Africa."

5. Notice if you experience any sensations in your body when you make a statement that you know to be false. Experiment with other false statements until you get a sense for what your body's signal for 'no' is. If you don't get a signal the first time you try this exercise, don't worry. Check to see if you are feeling really comfortable physically. Perhaps you can try again lying down.

6. Next, verbally make *true* statements about yourself. For example, I would say "I am a wom-

29

an," and, "I live in Canada." As you practice, notice any sensations in your body when you make your true statements. Keep experimenting until you get a sense for what your body's signal for 'yes' is.

7. Starting with simple statements helps to set the foundation so you can recognize your body's signals for 'no', for when a situation or interaction with another person arises in the future doesn't feel right. Some people call this your sixth sense.

As you interact with people, notice how your body responds to different people and situations, the more you practice connecting to your gut and noticing how you feel, the better you will get to know yourself and the messages from your body.

Exercise Seven

How often have you stopped to question your beliefs to examine if they are really true? By examining your beliefs and challenging them, you have the ability to change them, therefore producing different results based on your expectations.

Find a time and place where you can focus. Try to complete the exercise in its entirety. If it feels overwhelming, complete Step 1 and focus on ONE section of beliefs, before proceeding to step 9 and 10 (review and evaluation).[1]

---

1   Beliefs exercise taken from Coaching Horizons course manual, Become a Body Mind Spirit Coach, Barb Pierce.

Step 1: Write down ten significant **traumatic** and ten **empowering** events from your childhood. Write as quickly as you can without pausing to analyze your responses.

Traumatic Events

_____

_____

_____

_____

_____

_____

_____

_____

_____

_____

_____

_____

_____

Empowering Events

_____

_____

_____

_____

_____

_____

_____

_____

_____

_____

_____

_____

_____

_____

_____

_____

Step 2: Write down your beliefs about work (try to fill the page).

Here are some examples to guide you:

- Work should be fulfilling as we spend a lot of time doing it.
- Work is my way of contributing to the world.
- Work is stressful. Stress is needed in order to get ahead. (Limiting belief)
- I believe that my coworkers like me.
- I like that work is close to my home, reducing commute time as my time is important.

_____

_____

_____

_____

_____

_____

_____

_____

_____

_____

_____

_____

Step 3: Write down your beliefs about sex (try to fill the page). Write as quickly as you can without pausing to analyze.

_____

_____

_____

_____

_____

_____

_____

_____

_____

_____

_____

_____

_____

_____

_____

_____

_____

Step 4: Write down your beliefs about family (try to fill the page). Write as quickly as you can without pausing to analyze.

_____

_____

_____

_____

_____

_____

_____

_____

_____

_____

_____

_____

_____

_____

_____

_____

_____

Step 5: Write down your beliefs about friends (try to fill the page). Write as quickly as you can without pausing to analyze.

Step 6: Write down your beliefs about friends (try to fill the page). Write as quickly as you can without pausing to analyze.

_____

_____

_____

_____

_____

_____

_____

_____

_____

_____

_____

_____

_____

_____

_____

_____

_____

_____

Step 7: Write down any other beliefs about life that you have. These are beliefs that are not covered in any of the categories above.

_____

_____

_____

_____

_____

_____

_____

_____

_____

_____

_____

_____

_____

_____

_____

Step 8: Try and write even more of your beliefs — beyond the obvious, everyday ones — to the ones that may not be top of mind but that drive your behaviours in subtle ways.

Step 9: Review, evaluate and reset.

When you feel that you are done, go back and review your lists. For each area, identify which beliefs are true and which beliefs are 'limiting beliefs'—beliefs that are artificially holding you back from fully living your life. This portion of the exercise helps you to reconsider these limiting beliefs and offers you ways to begin changing the way you think about these areas of your life.

Limiting belief:

Work is stressful. Stress is needed in order to get ahead.

How my limiting belief has affected me:

I have become stressed at work by taking on too much in order to prove myself and have allowed it to interfere in my personal life and health by feeling grumpy, tired, and frustrated.

New belief:

Work does not need to be stressful.

List any new skills or resources required to make this belief change:

I will notice when I'm feeling stressed or frustrated and will challenge my thought pattern. There will be help available and a solution is possible if I ask for help. When I ask for help, I can solve problems sooner and I do not take the stress home with me, nor allow it to interfere with my personal life or health.

Continue going through the exercises for each limiting belief you have identified and write out your new belief, and then identify any resources or skills to make this belief change.

Step 10: Reflection.

Did you notice any patterns or receive insights from your childhood traumatic and empowering experiences that have had an impact on your beliefs now? What beliefs do you have that may not be 100% true? How would your life be better if you were living it based on the new empowering beliefs?

_____

_____

_____

_____

_____

_____

_____

_____

_____

_____

_____

_____

_____

_____

Exercise Eight

I suggest creating a daily ritual to acknowledge things in your life that you are thankful for. Whether you are thinking about things to be grateful for or writing a list each day, this should only take up a few minutes of your time. If you are stuck on what to be grateful for, start with simple things, such as the smell of the ocean, the warm sun on your face, your child's smile. Once you start finding things you are grateful for, you will be able to get more specific and your list will grow.

Following are some ways to practice gratitude – try them out to see what resonates, or create your own way:

1. Find a visual representation of something or someone whom you are grateful for and place this in a spot where you will see it every day, for example on your bedside table or your fridge. When you see this image or word, pause for a moment to take it in and enjoy the positive feelings in your body that this image generates.

2. Keep a gratitude journal. Each morning, or before you go to bed at night, take a few minutes to write in your journal, three things that you are grateful for. After practicing this for a while, you may even wish to expand the list beyond three.

3. Call up an old friend or family member, someone whom you haven't spoken to in a while and tell her something about her that you appreciate. It may surprise you how much of an impact this can have on a person.

4. Take the previous suggestion one step further and make a list of the important people in your

life. When was the last time you complimented them or shared why you value their presence? Make a date to call, email or text each person on your list, to say something nice and to let him or her know you are thinking of them and you are grateful to have them in your life.

5. Going even further, think of a difficult person in your life and reflect on a particular situation in which you may have been upset or angry with this person. Now that you can examine the bigger picture, ask yourself, what lesson did this person help teach you about yourself? Can you find gratitude from a difficult interaction? It's up to you whether or not you wish to reach out to this person to say thank you.

6. Last but not least, appreciate and have gratitude for yourself. You often are hardest on yourself and the most challenging task could be to appreciate your own qualities. You may wish to journal about this. If you're having trouble getting started, think of a time when you did something really well, or were praised by another person. What qualities did you exhibit that this person thought were great? Think of a time when you felt joy or happiness. What was it about that situation that you contributed to? Focusing on and appreciating your strengths, rather than focusing on what you think you're not good at, helps you to cultivate more of the positive traits and behaviour into your life.

Reflections

Exercise Nine

If you've been feeling that your life has been lacking in playfulness or joy lately, I encourage you to focus on the things that make you happy and make a commitment to yourself to set aside time to do them – create your joy list.

1. In the space below, start writing a list of things that bring you happiness or joy, whether it's a fun activity or sport, or spending time with a particular person.

2. Come up with at least ten items. Then challenge yourself to come up with at least three more.

3. Review your list and put a date beside the last time you participated in each activity. If you can't remember, put a big question mark beside that item.

4. Now, take a closer look at your list. Is there anything on there that you could do right away or participate in more than once during the week? Maybe a small pleasure that doesn't cost anything, nor take up a lot of your time. If so then make a commitment to do this one thing today. There's no time like the present.

5. Keep going through your list and place a date beside each item on your list for when you will do that activity. Be realistic with your time, there's no need to schedule them all within the next week. If you're ultra organized, schedule time in your calendar and set a reminder so these activities take priority, along with the other obligations in your life.

6. Revisit this list from time to time and acknowledge when you are doing something fun for yourself. If, after a few weeks, you've noticed you've slipped into old habits and are no longer checking your joy list, then either recommit to yourself to start it up again, or find a

support buddy. Creating this list with a friend is a great way to keep the momentum going by encouraging each other and holding one another accountable for having fun.

Joy List

_____

_____

_____

_____

_____

_____

_____

_____

_____

_____

_____

_____

_____

_____

Exercise Ten

Meditation isn't solely about sitting still on your yoga mat. You can get yourself into a meditative state, connecting you to the present moment, when you are completely immersed in an activity; one that allows the mind to stop bouncing around from thought to thought. This exercise[1] encourages you to explore meditation as a movement, to really slow down and observe your surroundings. It can be done indoors or outdoors. I particularly enjoy the walking meditation outside, in nature.

You can try this with no particular intent or you may ask a question prior to beginning the exercise, and then let go of any expectation of an answer. Often when I ask a question, the answer is revealed at the end when I notice what I observed during the exercise.

1. Remember to put away your phone and eliminate any other distractions before you begin. You can try this exercise alone, or with a friend and you can discuss your observations afterwards.

2. If you have a question in mind, try to formulate your question as a single sentence, as simply as you can, sticking to one topic or question, rather than a narrative or series of questions bundled together.

3. Repeat your question out loud.

4. No matter where you are, commit to at least ten minutes of walking around in silence. You do not need to have a particular destination, allow yourself to wander.

5. Notice the feeling of your feet on the floor or the ground, walk slowly and deliberately

---

1   Exercise inspired by and used with permission from Barb Pierce of *Coaching Horizons*.

becoming aware of each step at first. This helps to slow the mind down and connect you to your physical body.

6. Observe your surroundings, making no judgments about what you are seeing.

7. Tune into your other senses, what smells, sounds, touch or taste do you notice? It's not necessary that you try to seek out a specific smell or sound, you are scanning your surroundings and taking them in.

8. After a period of time, or whenever you feel ready to stop walking, get out your journal and start jotting down whatever comes to mind first. If you're practicing with a friend, you may journal and/or discuss your observations with your friend. What did you observe during your walk? Did you notice particular patterns in the things you were paying attention to? How did you feel during the exercise? Tuning into your other senses, were there particular sounds or sensations you experienced?

By reviewing your experience with respect to your question, you may find that the answer or some hints to your question were revealed during your walk. For example, we practiced this exercise during a retreat where we had a group of students walk around in the park, one student asked the question about what her greatest personal block was, as she was feeling frustrated with herself and others. During the walk she was particularly drawn to a large rock in the park and could not seem to walk away from it. She noticed the trees and the birds and many other things, yet the rock dominated her experience. She attributed this rock to represent her own stubbornness in life and realized she had to begin to change this and become more free like the birds – this was a revelation for her. Her attitude and energy appeared to have changed for the duration of the retreat. She was more engaged with her surroundings and with the other participants; overall she seemed to be enjoying herself more.

There are no right or wrong answers in how you interpret the meaning of your own experiences for yourself, what's important is that you are willing to explore and allow the answers to be revealed.

Reflections

Exercise Eleven

You can seek guidance by asking a question of your body (your inner guide or intuition) on your own. I've done this exercise many times and some days the signals just aren't there or I'm too distracted. Most days the answers arrive with ease. It's important to keep trying and don't beat yourself up if your inner wisdom is not cooperating on a given day. See if you can have fun and experiment with it.

1. Find a time and space where it will be quiet when you will have no interruptions.
2. Either sitting or lying down, take a few relaxing breaths.
3. Ask your body for support in answering your question.
4. Ask your question. Try to keep the question short and simple, for example 'What do I need to know right now regarding looking for another job?' or 'What do I need to learn about my relationship with my brother?'
5. Close your eyes and focus on your breathing, taking slow, deep breaths. Be patient and wait for the answers to be revealed.

The answer may come in the form of a word, a thought or a symbol that comes to mind. You may experience a physical sensation in a certain part of your body. If you experience a physical sensation, allow yourself to focus in on that area. Imagine you are breathing into that area, noticing if the sensation passes or gets stronger. When you continue to ask questions, putting yourself into a state of inquiry, it opens you up to finding meaning in your situation, often leading to a solution, instead of focusing on the problem itself. Only you can assign meaning to the messages you are receiving.

Reflections

Exercise Twelve

If you have been following along with the exercises in this book, you have been taking lots of action steps to get to know yourself and your inner world, which is primarily what drives your outer world experience. Ultimately you are responsible for holding yourself accountable. You have the power to create the circumstances in your world for a joyful and abundant life. Now is the time to check in, to acknowledge how far you've come and to evaluate if there is a particular area that needs more attention.

1. Have you done all of the exercises in the book so far?
2. Have you done some of the exercises but have skipped a few?
3. If you have skipped some or all of the exercises in this book, ask yourself why. Be honest with yourself.

By completing the above exercise, you have already taken your next smallest action step. As you are taking more action steps it's important to recognize and celebrate your accomplishments on your journey. Acknowledge what is going well and celebrate milestones by treating yourself somehow. Life is a journey, not a destination, right?

Bonus Exercise

If you're thinking you would like to be of service but you're not sure where to start, begin by asking yourself some questions.

Here are some suggestions to help you get started:

1. You can start right away by asking of yourself what you have to offer. Make a list of your strengths to determine how you could best be of service to others.

2. Start small, do something nice for someone today that doesn't cost you anything. Commit to smiling to at least three strangers on the street and notice their reactions. Don't be offended or take it personally if someone doesn't smile back though! It's not about you.

3. If you are interested in volunteering with an organization, then reach out to your friends and family, or your tribe to let them know your intentions. I suggest you do your research on organizations you are interested to volunteer for by reading up on their website and requesting additional information. Ask to be connected with existing volunteers to find out about their experiences. It's important to find a place where you feel there is a good fit.

While we're not all born into the same circumstances, you have the power to change your circumstances. You have the ability to offer help to another, making life a little easier for that person. Imagine what's possible if we all gave just a little bit. I believe it's the small things that add up to make a big difference.

Reflections

Reflections

Reflections

Reflections

Reflections

www.ingramcontent.com/pod-product-compliance
Lightning Source LLC
Chambersburg PA
CBHW080552030426
42337CB00024B/4847

9 780995 257320